DISCARD

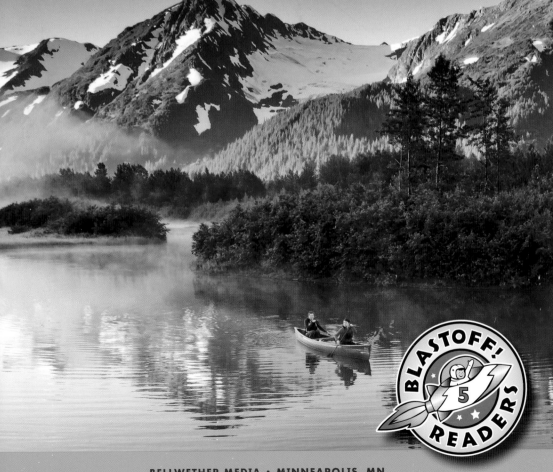

EXPLORING THE STATES
Alaska
THE LAST FRONTIER

by Emily Rose Oachs

BLASTOFF! 5 READERS

BELLWETHER MEDIA · MINNEAPOLIS, MN

Note to Librarians, Teachers, and Parents:

Blastoff! Readers are carefully developed by literacy experts and combine standards-based content with developmentally appropriate text.

Level 1 provides the most support through repetition of high-frequency words, light text, predictable sentence patterns, and strong visual support.

Level 2 offers early readers a bit more challenge through varied simple sentences, increased text load, and less repetition of high-frequency words.

Level 3 advances early-fluent readers toward fluency through increased text and concept load, less reliance on visuals, longer sentences, and more literary language.

Level 4 builds reading stamina by providing more text per page, increased use of punctuation, greater variation in sentence patterns, and increasingly challenging vocabulary.

Level 5 encourages children to move from "learning to read" to "reading to learn" by providing even more text, varied writing styles, and less familiar topics.

Whichever book is right for your reader, Blastoff! Readers are the perfect books to build confidence and encourage a love of reading that will last a lifetime!

This edition first published in 2014 by Bellwether Media, Inc.

No part of this publication may be reproduced in whole or in part without written permission of the publisher. For information regarding permission, write to Bellwether Media, Inc., Attention: Permissions Department, 5357 Penn Avenue South, Minneapolis, MN 55419.

Library of Congress Cataloging-in-Publication Data

Oachs, Emily Rose.
 Alaska / by Emily Rose Oachs.
   pages cm. – (Blastoff! readers. Exploring the states)
 Includes bibliographical references and index.
 Summary: "Developed by literacy experts for students in grades three through seven, this book introduces young readers to the geography and culture of Alaska"–Provided by publisher.
 ISBN 978-1-62617-001-8 (hardcover : alk. paper)
 1. Alaska–Juvenile literature. I. Title.
 F904.3.O24 2014
 979.8–dc23
                                                        2013002357

Text copyright © 2014 by Bellwether Media, Inc. BLASTOFF! READERS and associated logos are trademarks and/or registered trademarks of Bellwether Media, Inc. SCHOLASTIC, CHILDREN'S PRESS, and associated logos are trademarks and/or registered trademarks of Scholastic Inc.

Printed in the United States of America, North Mankato, MN.

Table of Contents

Where Is Alaska?

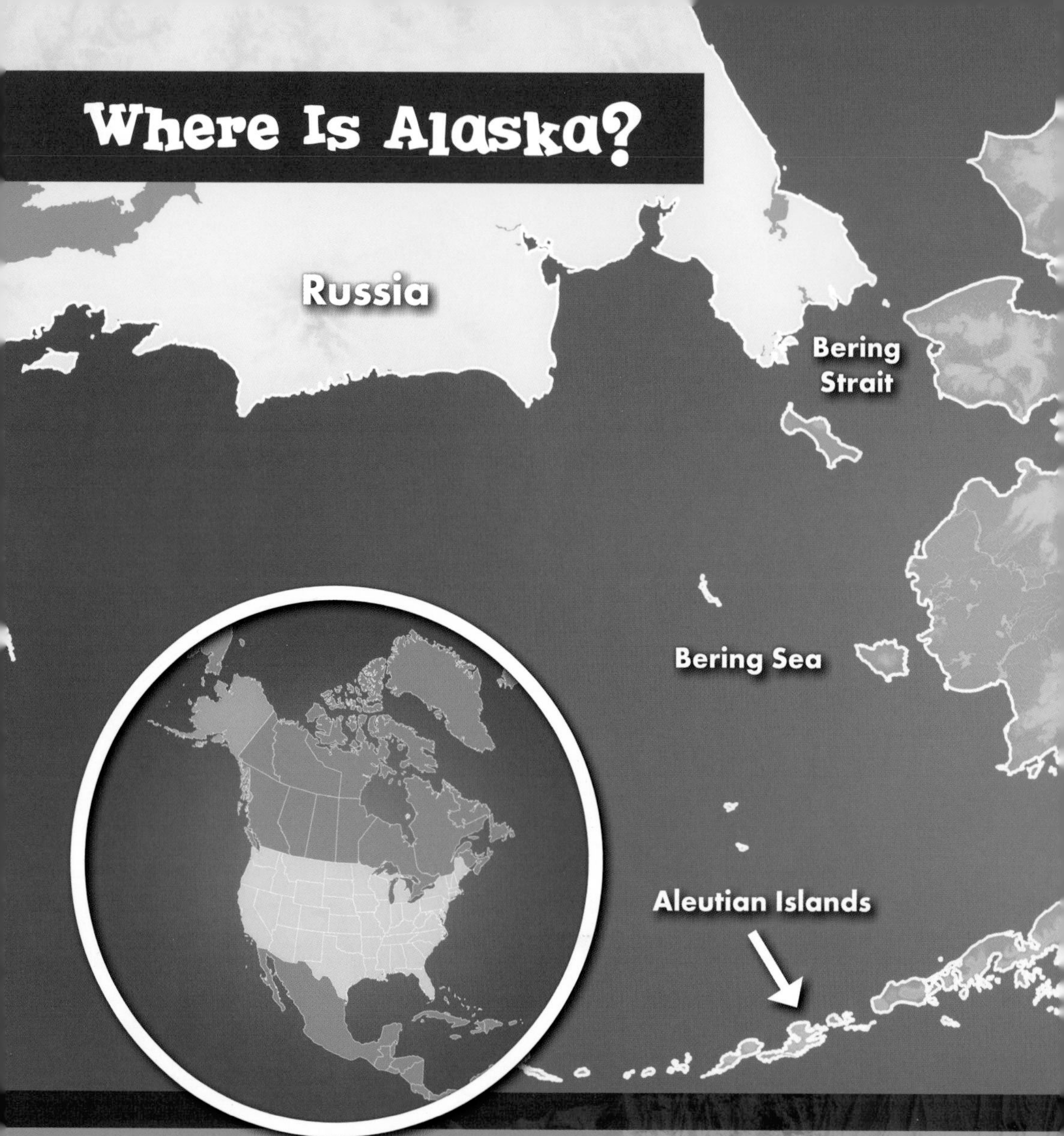

Russia

Bering Strait

Bering Sea

Aleutian Islands

Alaska is the largest state in the United States. It stretches over 590,693 square miles (1,529,888 square kilometers). Alaska is also the northernmost and westernmost state. It lies to the west of Canada and does not touch any other state. Alaska's capital is Juneau. This city is located near the Canadian border in the southeast.

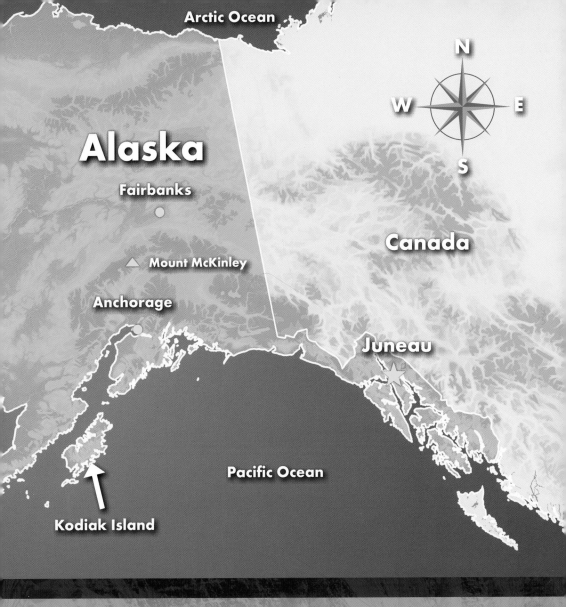

Arctic Ocean

Alaska

N
W   E
S

Fairbanks

Canada

▲ Mount McKinley

Anchorage

Juneau

Pacific Ocean

Kodiak Island

Alaska is a giant **peninsula**. The Arctic Ocean chills its northern coast while the Pacific Ocean touches its southern shores. To the west is the Bering Sea. Russia lies only about 50 miles (80 kilometers) across the Bering **Strait**. Alaska's Aleutian Islands also extend west toward this neighboring country.

History

The **native** peoples of Alaska came from Russia about 12,000 years ago. In 1741, Russia sent Vitus Bering to explore lands off the country's eastern coast. Bering became the first European to discover Alaska. He soon claimed the new land for Russia. Then in 1867, the United States purchased Alaska from Russia. Alaska became the forty-ninth state on January 3, 1959.

Did you know?

Native peoples made their homes in Alaska long before Europeans discovered it. Some of the first groups to live in Alaska were the Aleuts, Athabascans, Haida, Inuit, Tlingit, and Yupik.

Alaska Timeline!

1741:	**Vitus Bering discovers Alaska and claims it for Russia.**
1867:	**The United States pays Russia $7.2 million for Alaska.**
1906:	**Juneau becomes Alaska's capital.**
1942:	**Construction of the Alaska Highway is completed.**
1959:	**Alaska becomes the forty-ninth state.**
1964:	**A level 9.2 earthquake shakes Alaska. It is the strongest earthquake ever to hit North America.**
1968:	**Oil is discovered in northern Alaska.**
1975–1977:	**The Trans-Alaska Pipeline is built between Prudhoe Bay in the north and Valdez in the south.**
1989:	**The *Exxon Valdez* ship spills 11 million gallons of oil off Alaska's southern coast.**

Vitus Bering

Alaska Highway

Exxon Valdez

The Land

Mountains rise up from much of Alaska. **Glaciers** fill the mountain valleys. A **temperate rain forest** grows in the southeast. The Yukon River flows through the central lowlands to the Bering Sea. On the Aleutian Islands, **volcanoes** sometimes erupt.

Temperatures in Alaska range from mild in the southeast to below freezing in the north. In the far north lies the Arctic coastal **plain**, or North Slope. It sits within the frosty **Arctic Circle**. No trees can grow in the **permafrost** here. This flat landscape is known as the Arctic **tundra**.

fun fact !

In Alaska's far north, the summer sun does not set for as many as 84 days. This is called the "midnight sun."

Mount McKinley

Alaska's Climate
average °F

spring
Low: 3°
High: 31°

summer
Low: 43°
High: 64°

fall
Low: 1°
High: 21°

winter
Low: -28°
High: -7°

Did you know?
The Alaska Range is home to Mount McKinley. This is the highest peak in North America. It towers 20,320 feet (6,194 meters) above sea level.

Glaciers

Alaska is home to about 100,000 glaciers. These are giant masses of slowly moving ice. Glaciers form when layers of snow build up over hundreds of years. Over time, the top layers become so heavy that the snow on the bottom turns to ice.

Malaspina Glacier is the largest in the state. It is located in the Saint Elias Mountains in southeastern Alaska. Malaspina stretches over 1,500 square miles (3,885 square kilometers). In some places, it is over 1,000 feet (305 meters) thick.

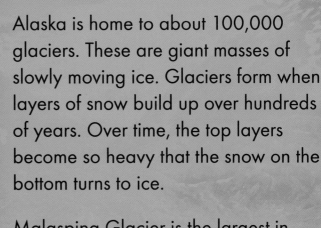

Malaspina Glacier

fun fact

Malaspina Glacier is one of the most massive glaciers in North America. It is bigger than the state of Rhode Island!

Wildlife

Alaska protects its wildlife in many national parks and **nature reserves**. Polar bears and caribou roam the tundra of the far north. Wolves and grizzly bears make their homes throughout the state. Black bears and moose thrive in the abundant forests. In the southeast, mountain goats and Dall sheep climb rugged peaks.

The coastal waters are filled with salmon, cod, and Alaska pollack. Beluga whales swim in the icy Arctic Ocean. In the Bering Sea, seals and walruses gather on sea ice. Peregrine falcons and horned puffins swoop and soar overhead.

Dall sheep

polar bear

beluga whale

! fun fact
More caribou than people live in Alaska! The state has about 950,000 caribou.

caribou

Landmarks

Alaska is known for its stunning scenery. Hundreds of thousands of **tourists** flock to Denali National Park each year to enjoy its untamed wilderness. Mount McKinley rises from the center of the park. Some visitors climb to its peak. Off the southern coast, Kodiak Island is rich in wildlife. It is home to the giant Kodiak bear. Visitors can also spot some 200 species of birds. The waters surrounding Kodiak Island are perfect for whale watching.

The Alaska Highway winds through beautiful natural countryside. It is the only route that connects Alaska's roads to Canada and the rest of the United States. The highway travels 1,523 miles (2,451 kilometers) to the city of Fairbanks.

Kodiak bear

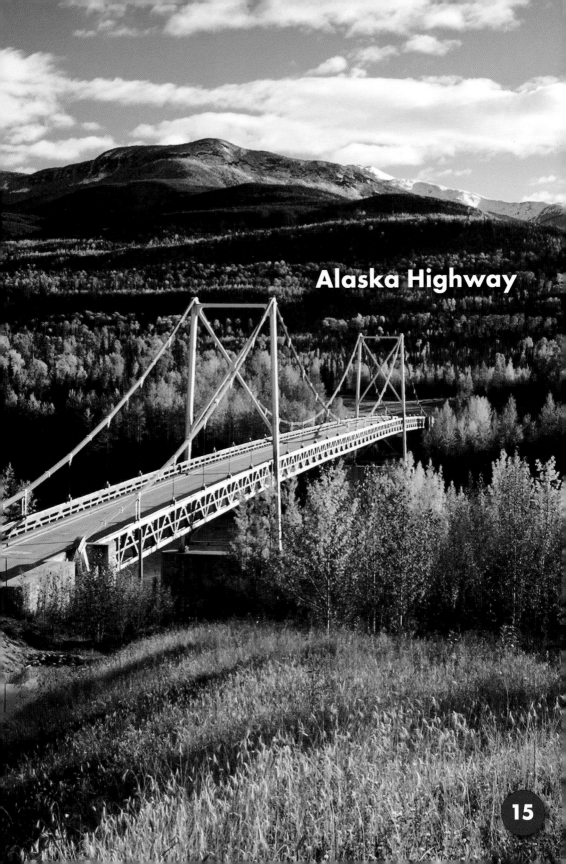

Alaska Highway

Juneau

Juneau was settled soon after gold was discovered there in 1880. It has been the capital of Alaska since 1906. Today, around 31,275 people call Juneau home. The city is built along the Gastineau **Channel** and nestled among mountains. To get to Juneau, people must travel by air or water. No roads lead to the city.

Did you know?
Juneau is the state capital, but Anchorage has more people. About half of Alaskans live in the Anchorage area.

Juneau Ice Field

Cruise ships carry thousands of tourists to Juneau's **port** every year. From there, they can explore nearby Glacier Bay or the Juneau Ice Field. Many also visit the Alaska State Museum in Juneau. It houses Alaskan **artifacts** and other items important to the state's history.

Working

Did you know?
When Alaska was purchased, some people thought it was a waste of money. The discoveries of gold, oil, and other resources proved Alaska was worth the $7.2 million.

fun fact

More than 1 million tourists visit Alaska each year.

Many Alaskans have **service jobs**. They work in schools, hospitals, and office buildings. Tourism also creates many service jobs. Alaskans work on cruise ships, as tour guides, and at national parks.

Natural resources are important to Alaska. The Trans-Alaska Pipeline carries oil 800 miles (1,287 kilometers) from northern to southern Alaska. Ships called tankers then bring it to other states. Workers mine gold, silver, coal, and natural gas. Fishers catch salmon, herring, halibut, and king crabs. Some farmers in western Alaska herd caribou. North of Anchorage, farmers grow potatoes, barley, and other crops.

Where People Work in Alaska

government
24%

farming and
natural resources
7%

manufacturing
3%

services
66%

Playing

Alaska's vast wilderness encourages many outdoor activities. Its mountains are great for climbing. Alaskans also enjoy bird-watching, hiking, and camping at state parks and nature reserves. Cross-country skiing and snowmobiling are popular during the long winters. Some people also go skijoring. A skier is pulled by a sled dog in this snow sport.

Every March, **mushers** and their dog teams compete in the Iditarod Trail Sled Dog Race. They travel over snow and ice for more than 1,100 miles (1,770 kilometers) from Anchorage to Nome. It takes most teams between 10 and 17 days to complete the journey.

fun fact !

Alaskans once used dogsledding as a form of transportation. Now dogsled racing is Alaska's state sport!

Food

Alaskan salmon

crab

Native Alaskans who lived near the coasts relied on the ocean for food. Aleuts and Inuit hunted walruses, whales, and seals. Tlingit caught salmon, herring, and other fish. Native Alaskans also gathered berries and hunted land animals such as caribou. Today, Alaskans continue to dine on salmon, crabs, and other seafood. Big **game** hunters also bring home bear, elk, caribou, and moose to eat.

Akutaq is sometimes called Eskimo ice cream. It is a tasty snack that native Alaskans brought on hunting trips. To make it, they mixed animal fat, ground fish, snow, and berries. Today, *akutaq* is made without animal fat and sweetened with sugar.

Akutaq

Ingredients:

1 large whitefish

1 cup Crisco

Sugar

Berries (blueberries or blackberries)

Directions:

1. Boil whitefish until done.

2. Debone fish and squeeze all liquid from fish so it is dry and fluffy.

3. Whip Crisco until fluffy. Add to fish and stir in well.

4. Add sugar to taste.

5. Add berries.

6. Keep cool or freeze.

Festivals

Alaska hosts many unique and fun festivals. Native peoples meet in Fairbanks for the World Eskimo-Indian Olympics each July. They compete in the four-man carry, the blanket toss, and other **traditional** events.

The Fur Rondy Festival takes place each February in Anchorage. The World Championship Sled Dog Race is the highlight of the event. Fairbanks hosts the World Ice Art Championships every March. Sculptors from around the world compete at carving ice blocks. Petersburg celebrates its Norwegian heritage with the Little Norway Festival in May. In late August, Alaskans gather in Palmer for the Alaska State Fair.

fun fact !

In the blanket toss, people pull a walrus skin tight. One person stands on the skin and is tossed into the air. The person must land without falling.

blanket toss

World Ice Art
Championships

Totem Poles

The Tlingit were among the first groups to live in Alaska. They settled along Alaska's southeastern coast. The Tlingit used wood in their villages to carve totem poles.

Totem poles are carved and painted for a specific reason. Many tell a story or **legend**. Some honor an important person who died. Others show a family's history. Eagles, bears, ravens, and beavers often appeared on the poles. Other native groups, such as the Haida and Tsimshian, also carved totem poles. These beautiful artifacts represent Alaska's connection to nature and tradition.

Fast Facts About Alaska

Alaska's Flag

Alaska's flag is deep blue with eight gold stars. The blue stands for Alaska's sky. The gold represents the state's resources. Seven of the stars form the Big Dipper. The North Star is in the upper right corner. It shows that Alaska is the northernmost state.

State Flower
forget-me-not

State Nicknames:	The Last Frontier Land of the Midnight Sun
State Motto:	"North to the Future"
Year of Statehood:	1959
Capital City:	Juneau
Other Major Cities:	Anchorage, Fairbanks
Population:	710,231 (2010)
Area:	590,693 square miles (1,529,888 square kilometers); Alaska is the largest state.
Major Industries:	fishing, mining, services, tourism
Natural Resources:	oil, natural gas, coal, silver, gold, zinc, fish, lumber
State Government:	40 representatives; 20 senators
Federal Government:	1 representative; 2 senators
Electoral Votes:	3

State Bird
willow ptarmigan

State Animal
moose

29

Glossary

Arctic Circle—a line that surrounds the North Pole; the land inside the Arctic Circle receives 24 hours of continuous daylight at least once a year.

artifacts—items made long ago by humans; artifacts tell people today about people from the past.

channel—a narrow body of water between two landmasses

game—wild animals hunted for food or sport

glaciers—massive sheets of ice that cover a large area of land

legend—a story from the past; legends are widely accepted but cannot be proven as fact.

mushers—dogsled drivers

native—originally from a specific place

natural resources—materials in the earth that are taken out and used to make products or fuel

nature reserves—lands that are set aside to preserve animal homes and to keep wildlife safe

peninsula—a section of land that extends out from a larger piece of land and is almost completely surrounded by water

permafrost—ground that is frozen year-round

plain—a large area of flat land

port—a sea harbor where ships can dock

service jobs—jobs that perform tasks for people or businesses

strait—a narrow stretch of water that connects two larger bodies of water

temperate rain forest—a forest of evergreen and broadleaf trees that receives a lot of rain; temperate rain forests grow in places with mild temperatures.

tourists—people who travel to visit another place

traditional—relating to a custom, idea, or belief handed down from one generation to the next

tundra—frozen, treeless land

volcanoes—holes in the earth; when a volcano erupts, hot, melted rock called lava shoots out.

To Learn More

AT THE LIBRARY

Miller, Debbie S. *Survival at 40 Below*. New York, N.Y.: Walker & Company, 2010.

Sandler, Martin W. *The Impossible Rescue*. Somerville, Mass.: Candlewick Press, 2012.

Shahan, Sherry. *Ice Island*. New York, N.Y.: Delacorte Press, 2012.

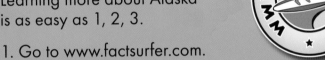

ON THE WEB

Learning more about Alaska is as easy as 1, 2, 3.

1. Go to www.factsurfer.com.

2. Enter "Alaska" into the search box.

3. Click the "Surf" button and you will see a list of related Web sites.

With factsurfer.com, finding more information is just a click away.

Index

The images in this book are reproduced through the courtesy of: Michael DeYoung/ Glow Images, front cover (bottom); Michael Sewell/ Getty Images, p. 6; WithGod, p. 7 (left); Calliopejen/ Wikipedia, p. 7 (middle); NOAA.gov, p. 7 (right); John R. Delapp/ Alaska Stock-Design Pics/ SuperStock, pp. 8-9; Mark Kelley/ Alaska Stock-Design Pics/ SuperStock, pp. 10-11; Mint Images-Frans Lanting/ Getty Images, p. 11; Wayne Lynch/ Glow Images, pp. 12-13; Luna Vandoorne, p. 12 (left); Iakov Filimonov, p. 12 (middle); Howard Sandler, p. 12 (right); Wildnerdpix, p. 14; Danny Xu, pp. 14-15; Kevin G. Smith/ Alaska Stock-Design Pics/ SuperStock, pp. 16-17; Imagebroker. net/ SuperStock, p. 17; Alaska Stock/ Alamy, p. 18; Konrad Wothe/ Glow Images, p. 19; Dmitry Kalinovsky, pp. 20-21; Anna Hoychuk, p. 22 (top); Michael Phillips, p. 22 (bottom); Associated Press, p. 23; Clark James Mishler/ Glow Images, p. 24; Gary Whitton, pp. 24-25; Don Pitcher/ Glow Images, pp. 26-27; Trubach, p. 28 (top); Gergo Orban, p. 28 (bottom); Majusko95, p. 29 (left); Agustin Esmoris, p. 29 (right).